EARTH'S RESOURCES

COAL

NEIL MORRIS

W

FRANKLIN WATTS

LONDON•SYDNEY

 An Appleseed Editions book

First published in 2005 by Franklin Watts
96 Leonard Street, London, EC2A 4XD

Franklin Watts Australia
Level 17/207 Kent Street, Sydney, NSW 2000

Created by Appleseed Editions Ltd,
Well House, Friars Hill, Guestling, East Sussex,
TN35 4ET

Designed by Guy Callaby

ISBN 0 7496 5988 2

A CIP catalogue for this book is available from the
British Library.

Photographs by Corbis (James L. Amos, Bettmann,
Andy Butler; Eye Ubiquitous, Dean Conger,
Margaret Courtney-Clarke, Bennett Dean; Eye
Ubiquitous, DK Limited, FK PHOTO, Lowell
Georgia, Chinch Gryniewicz; Ecoscene, Lindsay
Hebberd, E.O. Hoppé, Hulton-Deutsch Collection,
Larry Lee Photography, Lester Lefkowitz, John
Madere, Will & Deni McIntyre, Richard T. Nowitz,
Owaki – Kulla, Javier Pierini, Charles E. Rotkin, Bob
Rowan; Progressive Image, Royalty-Free, Rykoff
Collection, Alan Schein Photography, H. David
Seawell, Michael St. Maur Sheil, Paul A. Souders,
Vince Streano, Tim Wright, Felix Zaska), Getty
Images (David Hiser, Paul Sisul, Harry Taylor),
Photo Researchers, Inc. (Ludek Pesek)

Printed in Thailand

CONTENTS

INTRODUCTION   4

WHERE IN THE WORLD?   6

HOW COAL WAS FORMED   8

DIFFERENT TYPES OF COAL   10

EARLY HISTORY   12

STEAM POWER   14

SURFACE MINING   16

UNDERGROUND MINES   18

GENERATING ELECTRICITY   20

INDUSTRIAL RESOURCE   22

TRANSPORTING COAL   24

ENVIRONMENTAL PROBLEMS   26

TODAY AND TOMORROW   28

GLOSSARY   30

INDEX   32

INTRODUCTION

Coal is a black or dark brown rock that is found underground. It is made up mainly of carbon – the element that also forms diamonds. But coal was formed in a very different way to gemstones and other minerals.

When you look at a piece of coal, you might not guess that it originally came from plants that lived on Earth hundreds of millions of years ago. People had no idea of this in ancient times, but they soon came to realize that this remarkable substance could be very useful. It is a valuable source of energy, because when coal burns it gives off great heat. This has made it useful for warming houses and other buildings and it is also used in factories. Coal was once the main source of energy in industrial countries and it remains a most important resource today.

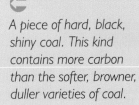

A piece of hard, black, shiny coal. This kind contains more carbon than the softer, browner, duller varieties of coal.

Fossil fuel

Because it comes from the fossilized remains of prehistoric plants, coal is called a fossil fuel. The world's other fossil fuels are oil and natural gas. We are using all three of these resources up at a very fast rate, and they all cause pollution to the environment when they are burned. Because of this, people who are concerned about the environment are encouraging scientists and governments to find new, alternative sources of energy. The material that was formed so many millions of years ago is no longer so popular in many parts of the world. Yet the worldwide production of coal keeps increasing every year.

Plant fossils, such as this seed, are often found in coal. They have taught experts a great deal about prehistoric plants.

Coal fires are not always easy to light. In homes, people first lit paper and sticks of wood before putting coal on top.

Coal fires

Before people in the world's wealthy countries had central heating, coal fires were common in most houses. From the middle of the 19th century until the mid-20th century in Britain, for example, people had fuel delivered to their door by a coalman. They bought large sacks of the fuel, which they stored in a coalhole or coalhouse. Fires were lit in the main rooms of the house, and coal was also used in the kitchen to heat up the oven for cooking. This made for hard work, especially since burning coal leaves behind ashes, which had to be cleared away every day.

WHERE IN THE WORLD?

Coal is found on all of the world's continents and is mined on all of them except Antarctica. That is because there is an international agreement banning mining on the frozen continent.

There are also coal deposits beneath the oceans, but they are too difficult and expensive to mine. Experts believe that there are large reserves of coal in about 70 countries around the world. More coal is produced annually today than was ever produced in the past. Today, the greatest amounts of coal are mined in China, which produces more than a third of the world's total. The next largest producer is the United States, followed by India.

These miners are loading coal into baskets at a mine in the state of Assam, in northeastern India. Many of India's deposits of coal are near Earth's surface.

Big lumps of coal are put into trucks, ready to leave Datong.

This old colliery in South Wales was busy producing coal during the 20th century. Now it is a popular museum.

Datong, China

The Datong region of Shanxi province, in northeast China, is one of the biggest coal-producing areas of the world's largest coal-producing country. Datong was founded as a fortified settlement in the fourth century and soon became the capital of the Buddhist Northern Wei dynasty. Coal mining developed rapidly there in the 1920s, and today there are 15 coal mines in the Datong region. The city of Datong itself has more than a million inhabitants, and many people work in the local factories, which produce cement, railway equipment, farm machinery, processed food and shoes.

Coalville, UK

Miners started digging coal at the Snibston colliery, in the English county of Leicestershire, in 1833. A railway constructed by engineer Robert Stephenson connected Snibston to the Leicester-Swannington line built by his famous father, George Stephenson. Miners' houses near the colliery grew into a settlement that was officially named Coalville. Coal was produced there for 150 years, but in 1983 the pit finally closed down. Today the town of Coalville has a population of 33,000, but coal is no longer produced there.

HOW COAL WAS FORMED

The coal that we use today was formed long before the first humans appeared on Earth. Most of it began to form during a time that we call the Carboniferous Period, sometimes referred to as the 'Age of Coal Forests'.

This period lasted from about 360 to 286 million years ago, when large, swampy forests covered the land. Giant ferns and other plants lived in the swamps, and when they died they fell into the warm, shallow water and started to decay. New plants grew over the decaying vegetation, which piled up and was pressed tightly together by the material on top of it. Over a long period of time, the pressure turned the vegetation into a spongy mass called peat. This process was repeated over and over until the water was squashed out of the peat and it turned into coal.

 This is what a Carboniferous coal swamp would have looked like.

Peat

Today there are peat deposits throughout the world, and there are especially large peat bogs in Canada and Finland. Peat has been used for many centuries as a fuel. The peat is dug by hand and then laid out in blocks to dry before being stored for the winter. The ancient Romans did this in eastern England, causing the fens of present-day East Anglia to become much drier. In recent years, peat has become very popular with gardeners as a fertilizer. Unfortunately, mechanical diggers collecting peat for fertilizer can soon destroy a peat bog. In order to protect the bogs and allow them to develop further, gardeners in many countries are now encouraged to use peat-free composts.

Digging and drying peat on a small scale, as people have traditionally done in Ireland, is not harmful to the environment.

These modern tree ferns, growing in New Zealand, are similar to those that formed part of the ancient coal forests.

The world's wetlands

Swamps, marshes, bogs – they are all wetlands, or areas of land with waterlogged soil. They form ideal conditions for the formation of peat and eventually coal, but this process takes millions of years. They give us the opportunity to see what the world was like many millions of years ago. Wetlands also form ideal habitats for many different plants and all kinds of wildlife. Many of the world's wetlands are in danger, as developers want to drain them to make rich farmland. Some wetlands, such as part of the huge Okefenokee Swamp in Georgia, have been turned into wildlife refuges and national parks.

DIFFERENT TYPES OF COAL

There are three main types of coal, which vary in age and depth underground. All three types occur in layers, and they are often sandwiched between different kinds of rocks, such as sandstone or shale.

The first stage in the formation of coal is when weight and pressure turns peat into lignite, which is soft and crumbly. The next stage, deeper down, is made up of bituminous coal (from the Latin word *bitumen*, a kind of tarry pitch). This is also called soft coal, although it is much harder and drier than lignite. It is the most commonly found kind of coal and is mostly used in factories. The deepest level produces a very black, glossy kind of coal called anthracite. This is the driest kind of coal and gives off the most heat. The different coals are also ranked according to the amount of carbon they contain. Some lignite contains only about 30 per cent carbon, while the highest-ranking anthracite contains up to 98 per cent.

These samples show the layers of coal – from the bottom: anthracite, bituminous, and lignite – with a layer of peat and living plants on top.

Lignite

The name 'lignite' comes from the Latin word for wood; it is also known as 'brown coal' because of its colour. You can often see traces of the original plants in this woody substance. Germany produces more lignite than any other country, followed by Russia and the US. Because it is less dry and contains less carbon than harder coals, it produces less heat. Lignite also gives off more carbon dioxide gas than other coals, and many environmentalists feel that it should not be used as a fuel.

 This land, near Leipzig in Germany, was once the site of a lignite mine. Now it is being returned to its natural state.

 This postcard from 1944 shows a plant in the 'Anthracite Region' of eastern Pennsylvania. Large chunks of anthracite were broken into small lumps, which were known locally as 'black diamonds'.

Anthracite

The name 'anthracite' comes from the Greek word for coal; it is also known as 'hard coal'. It is the least plentiful kind of coal, with much of it produced by China and South Africa. Anthracite is valued as a fuel for open fires in homes because it burns slowly with a clean flame and gives off less smoke than other kinds of coal. In the days when houses were heated by fireplaces, people would often burn cheaper bituminous coal, which was easier to light, along with the more expensive anthracite that burned better and for longer.

EARLY HISTORY

In about 350 BC, the ancient Greek philosopher and scientist Aristotle wrote a book about Earth's weather conditions called Meteorologica. In it, he mentioned rocks that looked like charcoal that could catch fire and burn.

The rocks were found in southern and eastern Europe, and this may be the first written reference to coal. But people might have been burning coal much earlier than this. Archaeologists believe that coal was burned to make funeral pyres up to 4,000 years ago in northern Europe. Coal was certainly prized and used by the ancient Romans after they invaded Britain. They found it near Hadrian's Wall in the county of Northumberland and transported it to their towns further south. By AD 1200, coal was being used in North America too. The Hopi people of present-day Arizona picked and scraped coal in dry valleys, using it for heating and sometimes for firing pottery.

A modern example of a traditional Hopi pot. About 800 years ago, the Hopi Native Americans found coal and started using this instead of wood to fuel their kilns and fire clay pots.

Coal was among the many treasures that Marco Polo found in use in China. Others included ivory, jade, porcelain and silk.

Ancient China

When he returned to Venice in 1295 after his long journey to China, the great Italian traveller Marco Polo described many of the amazing things that he had seen in the Far East. He wrote that throughout northern China, people dug a sort of black stone out of the mountains and that, when they were lit, the stones burned throughout the night and gave off great heat. The 'black stones' – lumps of coal – had in fact been mined in China since around 1,000 BC, when they were probably first used for smelting copper and then for casting coins.

Sea coal

During the 13th century, coal was also mined in Britain, especially in northeastern England. Some of the first English coal may have come from the coast, where rocky lumps had been washed up from exposed coal veins by the powerful action of the sea. This might be the reason that the British referred to it as 'sea coal', although Londoners may have invented the term because their coal arrived by sea from Northumberland. Many people still liked to burn wood in their homes, because they preferred the smell to that of coal fires, which were more smoky and sooty. But as English forests were cut down and began to disappear, coal was used more and more.

This photograph from 1939 shows a woman collecting sea coal on the Northumberland coast.

STEAM POWER

By the late 17th century, Britain was producing more than three-quarters of the world's coal. Much of it was used in the factories that were springing up all over the country. Wood had become scarce and was simply replaced by coal.

In the 18th century, the technological changes that took place in the factories brought about a change in society that is known as the Industrial Revolution. This could not have come about without the invention of the steam engine, which needed coal to heat water and turn it into steam. In 1712, an English blacksmith named Thomas Newcomen invented a steam engine that was used to pump water out of mines. Fifty-seven years later, Scottish engineer James Watt improved on this, and by the 19th century, steam engines were being used to power locomotives and ships.

In James Watt's steam engine, a coal furnace heated water into steam, which was used to push a piston, which rocked a beam and turned a flywheel. This power was then used to work machines.

Smelting iron

Just as coal replaced wood for heating homes, a form of coal called coke came to be used for smelting iron. Coke was made by heating coal in an airtight oven, and in 1709 (three years before Newcomen invented his steam engine), English iron-maker Abraham Darby converted a furnace to burn coke instead of charcoal. It worked brilliantly and made iron cheaper and easier to produce. Along with coal and steam, iron also became an important element in the Industrial Revolution.

The great number of factories meant that smoke was belched out over growing industrial cities.

Rocketing along

In 1804, an English engineer named Richard Trevithick built the first steam locomotive, which pulled cars in an ironworks. Just over 20 years later, steam trains were carrying the world's first railway passengers. The locomotives required a great deal of coal to keep their boilers working, so a special car called a tender was attached behind the engine. A fireman had to keep shovelling coal into the firebox to stoke the boiler and maintain a constant supply of steam. It was hard work, but it brought results. By 1830, the successful *Rocket* locomotive could travel at up to 29 miles per hour, which was amazingly fast for the time.

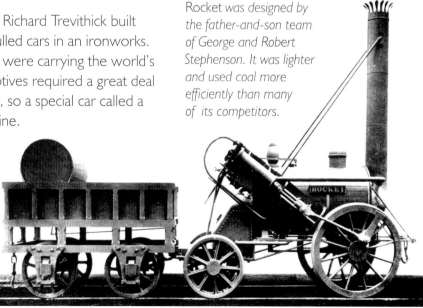

Rocket was designed by the father-and-son team of George and Robert Stephenson. It was lighter and used coal more efficiently than many of its competitors.

SURFACE MINING

Coal is found in layers called seams. Some seams are just 2.5 centimetres wide, while others may be more than 100 metres wide. Coal seams are often separated by layers of other rocks, and many layers have been bent and folded over millions of years as mountains and valleys have been formed by movements in the earth.

Some coal seams are found in horizontal layers close to the Earth's surface. The soil and rock that lie above such a coal seam, known as the overburden, can be removed in so-called opencast or open-pit mines. The overburden is often removed in strips by enormous digging machines, which is why the process is sometimes called 'strip mining'. Sometimes drills and explosives are used to break up surface rocks, and opencast mines might recover coal deposits as deep as 60 metres.

This enormous electric shovel moves along slowly on caterpillar tracks. It strips the surface so that coal can be dug up from below.

Multi-seams and high walls

Most open pits are located where there are several coal seams near the surface. These modern multi-seam pits are much more successful and profitable than old single-seam mines. Some of the huge cutting machines are operated by remote control, making the work more precise and safer. At the Moura mine in Queensland, Australia, miners use special cutting machines that can work on thick seams and leave high walls as the coal is removed. The mine, which was started in 1961, employs more than 470 people and produces more than 5 million tonnes of coal every year.

 A big rotary digger can also be used for recovering coal at the surface.

 Huge trucks and loaders are used to take the coal away at an open pit.

Computerized coalface

If the land above a coal seam is hilly, machines are used to cut wide ledges into the hillside. In modern mines, computers use satellites as a positioning system so that the digging machines and mining shovels can be moved to exactly the right place. Such a system is used at the Greenhills Mine in the Canadian Rocky Mountains of British Columbia. There the coal seams were folded as the mountains formed, and some of the open pits started by taking the tops off of the mountains.

UNDERGROUND MINES

To recover coal from deep seams, shafts are dug from the surface. In slope mines, the shafts are dug at an angle, and in drift mines they lead horizontally into a mountain.

But vertical shafts lead to the deepest mines, and workers and equipment are lowered down by lift. Horizontal tunnels lead off the shafts to the coal seams. In the room-and-pillar system, the coal is cut out in spaces, or 'rooms', with pillars of coal left standing to support the tunnel roof. Mechanical cutters gouge out the coal, and conveyor belts carry it to one of the main shafts. When enough of the seam has been mined, the pillars are removed, and the rooms are allowed to collapse after the miners and equipment have all moved back to a main shaft.

Companies keep modern mines working day and night. The tall buildings are winding houses, which hold the cables that work the lifts for miners and haul up coal skips, or buckets.

Longwall mining

Many underground mines now use a different system to cut long seams of coal. The coal is mined from one long face by a powerful cutting machine, or shearer. Steel props support the roof over the face, which is allowed to collapse behind the miners and the machine as they move forward. Some coalfields started off being mined by the room-and-pillar method but have recently switched to the longwall method, which can be more productive.

In the old days

Underground mining was always a hard, dangerous way of life. Before machines or even drills were introduced, miners had to hack away at the coalface with picks and shovels. They worked in dark, dusty conditions and had to rely on wooden props to hold up tunnel roofs. Before the invention of the safety lamp in 1815, naked flames were used to light the tunnels, and they often caused explosions. Miners did not wear masks, and many suffered from lung diseases. Centuries ago, young children were sent down into the mines because they were small and could move more easily through narrow tunnels.

The spinning teeth of a longwall shearer cut off bits of coal that are carried away on a conveyor belt.

This photograph suggests what life was like for coal miners years ago.

GENERATING ELECTRICITY

Today, the main use of coal is for generating electricity. Coal produces more than a third of the world's electrical power, and this uses up about half of the coal mined every year.

Some countries use more natural gas, nuclear power, water power or oil, but coal generates more than three-quarters of the electricity needed by Australia, China, India, Poland, and South Africa. Half of the US's enormous demand for electricity is met by coal, while in the UK the figure is about a third. The electricity is made by huge generators in power stations, which deliver it to power lines connected to homes and factories. The first plant of this kind was the Pearl Street power station in New York, which started making electricity in 1882.

A coal-fired power station in Greece. The electricity produced by its generators is delivered to towns and cities along power lines held high above the ground on pylons. The four structures on the right are cooling towers, where unused steam turns back into water.

When the coal is burned, it gives off smoke and gases through tall chimneys.

Inside the power station, steam drives the blades of turbines. These turn the rotors of the generators seen here.

Releasing energy

By burning coal, power stations release the energy that has been locked up underground for many millions of years. But the coal is not just burned in lumps as it would be in a fireplace at home. First it is ground into a fine powder in a milling machine called a pulverizer. Then the coal powder is blown by hot air into a boiler, where it burns at about 1,400° centigrade. This heats water to boiling point, creating the steam that drives the turbine and generator. A large power station uses several million tons of coal every year. Such plants mostly use bituminous coal, which has the highest heating value.

Power location

In 1882, the Pearl Street power station served only a small section of New York's Manhattan district. Yet huge amounts of coal had to be transported to the plant. Today, many power stations are built closer to the source of their fuel. In China, the Yancheng plant started producing electricity in 1999. It is built beside a coal mine and transmits electricity to another province 740 kilometres away. It is easier and cheaper to send the electricity long distances than it is the coal. This is sometimes called a 'coal-by-wire' strategy.

INDUSTRIAL RESOURCE

Coal is used as a fuel in many industries. To produce cement, for example, powdered coal is burned in a kiln to heat limestone, clay, and other materials up to 1,600° centigrade and turn them into a substance called clinker. This is ground into cement, which is then used to make concrete.

Other processes, such as iron- and steelmaking, use coke as fuel. Coke is made by heating powdered bituminous coal in an airtight oven, which changes some of the solids in the coal into gases. These gases can be used for other purposes, along with the coal tar that is also produced. The hot coke is cooled with water before being stored and used as a fuel. Some coal is also used to make gases by being treated in a process called gasification. This makes a gas that can be used as a heating fuel in industry, although it has the disadvantage of giving off a lot of soot as it burns.

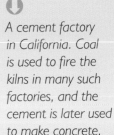

A cement factory in California. Coal is used to fire the kilns in many such factories, and the cement is later used to make concrete.

Iron and steel

Iron is made by smelting iron ore in a blast furnace, separating the metal from the rock. Coke and limestone are fed into the top of the furnace, along with the iron ore, and blasts of hot air are blown in. The coke burns, and the limestone combines with the rocky parts of the ore to make a grey material called slag. This leaves molten metal, which runs off at the bottom as so-called pig iron. The iron is re-melted and refined to make steel.

The molten steel is poured into a mill, where it is rolled into strips. The whole process of steelmaking begins in a blast furnace, where coke is used as the fuel.

These Kassena people of Ghana use coal tar to decorate mud huts with traditional patterns.

Dyes and mothballs

Coal tar and coke-oven gas are both by-products of the coke-making process. The sticky liquid known as coal tar can be used to make light oils, which in turn are used make dyes, perfumes, and antiseptics. In 1856, English chemist William Perkin developed the world's first man-made dye from coal-tar chemicals. This dye was called 'mauve' (from the French word for the mallow flower), and the term has since been used for a pale purple colour. Another coal-tar product is the chemical called naphthalene, which has a distinctive smell and is used to make mothballs.

TRANSPORTING COAL

Today, many of the world's mines are far away from the steelworks, power stations and other industrial plants that need coal. Within countries, most cargoes are carried in freight cars by rail or on large barges by river.

Major coal-exporting countries, such as Australia, China and Indonesia, send huge cargo ships between coastal ports and across the world's oceans. Every year, more than 570 million tonnes of coal are shipped around the world by sea. Specialist companies serve ports and terminals, often delivering coal in long trains that may be pulled by several locomotives, have more than 100 cars and be more than 1.6 kilometres long. For shorter distances, coal may even be mixed with water and pumped through underground pipes. In the US, a 430-kilometre pipeline carries coal from a mine in Arizona to a power plant in Nevada.

Coal freighters make long voyages across the world's oceans. They deliver their cargo to the ports of importing countries.

Sorting and washing

Coal is prepared and treated before it is transported from the mine. First the chunks of coal are sorted into different sizes. Large chunks are crushed into smaller lumps. Sorted coal is then washed in water tanks or sprayed with water to remove ash and other impurities. Finally, the wet coal passes through drying machines and hot-air blowers, since dry coal burns much better than wet coal.

A long coal train makes its way from a mine in New Mexico.

The docks at Newcastle upon Tyne, in north-east England, photographed in 1925. This British city was once a major center for coal production and shipping.

Carrying coal from Newcastle

Australia exports more coal than any other country. At major ports, such as Newcastle in New South Wales, there are special coal terminals. Coal was first discovered near Newcastle in 1797, and two years later a ship carried its first cargo of coal from there to India. At the beginning of the 21st century, the terminal loads more than 800 ships and handled up to 70 million tonnes of coal every year. Like other terminals it keeps huge stockpiles of coal on hand so that ships can load up immediately.

ENVIRONMENTAL PROBLEMS

One of the main problems with coal, as with all fossil fuels, is that it pollutes the air when it is burned. During the 20th century, many of the world's cities were choked with fumes from coal-burning factories, power plants and fires in homes. This resulted in laws being passed to cut down on the amount of pollution.

In London, for example, people were allowed to burn only smokeless fuels in their homes after the 1950s. The gases given off by burning coal, such as sulphur dioxide, cause many environmental problems. Factories are encouraged to use types of coal with a lower sulphur content. They have also installed devices called scrubbers, which filter and clean fumes as they pass through chimneys. At the Belle Vue power plant, on the Indian Ocean island of Mauritius, pulped sugar-cane is burned to fuel the boilers during the growing season. This harms the atmosphere less than the South African coal that is used during the rest of the year.

A coal-burning plant in Maryland. Power plants are often built near rivers or the coast, because they need water for steam and cooling.

Air pollution

Fumes from coal-fired power plants pollute the air for a great distance around the plant. Gases of sulphur and nitrogen drift high in the air from chimneys, and some dissolve in the water droplets that make up clouds. This makes acid rain, which damages lakes, rivers and forests when it falls on them. Many parts of eastern North America, Scandinavia and central Europe have been badly affected by acid rain, which has killed fish in lakes, damaged many thousands of trees and even polluted soil.

These trees have been damaged by acid rain, which has caused leaves and whole branches to die.

Climate change

Coal is made up of carbon. When coal is burned, it releases a gas called carbon dioxide. This gas is present naturally in the atmosphere and, along with other so-called greenhouse gases, it helps to soak up and trap heat that would otherwise radiate from Earth back out into space. But producing and releasing too much carbon dioxide makes the atmosphere trap more of the sun's heat, creating a 'greenhouse effect'. This has led to a gradual heating up of the world, and scientists fear that this global warming might lead to more floods, storms and a rise in sea levels as polar ice melts.

Along with car-exhaust fumes, the smoke and gases given off by coal-burning factories can choke our cities with smog (short for 'smoke fog').

TODAY AND TOMORROW

At the beginning of the 21st century, coal still provides almost a quarter of the world's energy needs. During the last century, the production of coal increased dramatically – by more than three times in the US, and by 20 times in China in the second half of the century alone.

But by 2000 some countries – such as France – were turning to other forms of energy, producing less coal and sometimes importing more. Experts predict that the world's known coal reserves will last for more than 200 years if we keep on mining and using coal at the same rate as today. Of course, it is possible that mining methods will continue to improve, and there may be more coal yet to be discovered. But once these supplies have been used up, they will not be replaced for thousands of millions of years to come. It seems that there is no long-term future for coal.

A stockpile of coal. Most of the world's reserves are in the U.S., Russia, and China.

Old mines

In April 2004, the last working coal mine in France closed down. France gradually reduced its production of coal during the 20th century, and by 2000 more than three-quarters of the country's energy was being produced by nuclear power plants. Some of the old mines have become museums and tourist attractions, as they have in other parts of the world. Even in countries that are still more dependent on coal, there are many fewer mineworkers, as the industry has become more mechanized. This trend will surely continue, so that much of the mining work is done by remote control.

Old coal mines make popular museums and attractions. This one in Canada was an important source of coal in the 19th and 20th centuries.

This wind farm is in California. The US is the world's biggest energy-user.

New alternatives

Coal and other fossil fuels will remain important for years to come, and China is expected to produce and use more and more coal over the next 50 years. But there are plenty of alternative energy sources too. These include solar energy (power from the sun), geothermal energy (from hot rocks beneath Earth's surface) and power provided by wind and waves. All of these are called renewable sources of energy, because the supplies renew themselves. Coal is a non-renewable resource, so we must look at all the alternatives for our future energy needs.

GLOSSARY

anthracite A very black, glossy kind of hard coal.

archaeologist A person who studies the ancient past by digging up and looking at remains.

bituminous coal A kind of soft coal that burns with a smoky flame.

blacksmith A person who makes and repairs iron objects.

charcoal A black form of carbon made by heating wood.

coal swamp A prehistoric swamp where dead vegetation eventually formed coal.

coke A solid fuel made from coal.

colliery A coal mine and its buildings.

compost A substance spread to make soil richer and more fertile.

continent One of Earth's seven huge land masses.

element A substance that cannot be separated into a simpler form.

environmentalist A person who is concerned about and acts to protect the natural environment.

fertilizer A substance spread to make soil richer and more fertile.

fossil The preserved remains of a prehistoric plant or animal.

fossil fuel A fuel (such as coal, oil or natural gas) that comes from the remains of prehistoric plants and animals.

fuel A substance that is burned to provide power or heat.

furnace An oven-like structure in which materials can be heated to very high temperatures.

gasification The process of producing gas from coal.

Industrial Revolution The rapid development of machinery, factories and industry that began in the late 18th century.

lignite A soft, crumbly kind of brown coal.

mineral A solid chemical substance that occurs naturally in the earth.

multi-seam pit A mine where several coal seams are dug up.

national park An area of land where wildlife and the environment are protected.

opencast or **open-pit mine** A mine in which coal is extracted at or near the surface of the earth.

overburden Soil and rock lying above a coal seam.

peat A spongy, wet mass of decomposed vegetation.

pig iron Crude iron obtained from a furnace.

pollution Damage to the environment caused by harmful substances.

pulverizer A milling machine that grinds coal into a powder.

room-and-pillar mine A mine in which large tunnels are dug and supported by pillars.

rotor The rotating part of a machine such as a generator.

scrubber A device that filters and cleans fumes as they pass through a chimney.

seam A layer of coal between layers of other rocks.

shearer A powerful coal-cutting machine.

slag Stony waste matter that is produced when ore is smelted.

smelt To heat and melt ore in order to get metal from it.

strip mining Stripping away soil and rock to expose and mine coal.

swamp An area of land that is always wet; it is known as a wetland.

tender A car holding coal and water for a steam locomotive.

vein A layer (of coal or ore) formed in a crack between rocks.

wetland An area of land with waterlogged soil.

INDEX

alternative energy sources 5, 29
ancient civilizations 9, 12, 13
  China 13
  Hopi 12
  Rome 9, 12
anthracite 10, 11
Aristotle 12

bitumen 10
blast furnaces 23

carbon 4, 10, 11, 27
carbon dioxide 11, 27
Carboniferous Period 8
cement 7, 22
coal
  'coal-by-wire' 21
  deposits 6, 9, 16
  formation 4, 5, 8, 9, 10
  home heating 11, 13, 15, 21, 26
  largest producers 6
  mining 6, 13, 16, 17, 18, 19
  processing 16, 22, 23, 25
  production 5, 28, 29
  reserves 6, 28
  transport 24, 25
  use in industry 22
Coalville, UK 7
coke 15, 22, 23

Darby, Abraham 15
Datong, China 7
diamonds 4
drills 16, 19
dyes 23

electricity 21, 22
environmental concerns 5, 26, 27
  global warming 27
  greenhouse gases 27
  pollution 5, 26, 27

factories 4, 7, 10, 14, 20, 26
fossil fuels 5, 26, 29

gasification 22

iron 15, 22, 23

lignite 10, 11

mines 6, 7, 13, 14, 16, 17, 18, 19, 29
  drift mines 18
  Greenhills Mine, Canada 17
  longwall mining 19
  Moura Mine, Australia 17
  room-and-pillar 18, 19
  shafts 18
  slope mines 18
  strip mining 16
  surface mining 16
  underground mines 18, 19

mothballs 23
museums 29

Newcastle, Australia 25

Okefenokee Swamp, USA 9

peat 8, 9, 10
Polo, Marco 13
power stations 20, 21, 24
  Pearl Street power station, New York 20, 21
pulverizers 21

sea coal 13
seams 15, 17, 18, 19
shearers 19
slag 23
smelting 13, 15, 23
steel 19, 22, 23

tourism 29
trains 14, 15
Trevithick, Richard 15

Watt, James 14